I Want To Be A Doctor

For Children & Youth

SYLVANUS UDO

Copyright © 2019 Sylvanus Udo

All rights reserved.

ISBN: 9781795594080

DEDICATION

To God Almighty.

CONTENTS

	Introduction	1
1	Chapter 1: **Who Is A Doctor**	3
2	Chapter 2: **Have A Vision**	7
3	Chapter 3: **Type Of Medical Doctors and Their Functions**	11
4	Chapter 4: **Medical Instrument And Their Uses**	21
5	Chapter 5: **Why Do People Consult Medical Doctors**	27
6	Chapter 6: **Importance And Duties Of Medical Doctors**	29
7	Chapter 7: **Common Illness, Diseases, Infections/Symptom Etc.**	37
8	Chapter 8: **Keys To Achieving What You Want**	43
9	Chapter 9: **Exercise on Human body**	47

ACKNOWLEDGMENTS

My appreciation goes to all who made this work a success.

Introduction

Often time young people say that they want to be a Doctor. It takes them few minutes to say what they want to become but they don't realize that it takes years to accomplish it. This book is to help young people understand, appreciate more, what it means and what it takes to become a Doctor or any other profession one want to venture into.

In some countries Education system, when a child starts school at age five in primary one, it takes six years to finish primary school. Junior secondary school is three years and senior secondary school is three years. The higher institution is four years. That is 6 3 3 4 system. In that of studying Medicine as a course it takes seven years depending on the area of studies.

To become a Doctor it requires focus, hard work, consistency and persistency. When young people say that they want to be a Doctor, I believe they refer to becoming Medical Doctors. Medical practice is very serious work because they deal with human body. It takes training for a child or anyone to become what they want to become in life, because there are no born medical doctor but trained Doctors. You can be what you want to be, if you work hard at it. Discover your purpose and follow it. When purpose is not revealed, life becomes a problem. Your years of youthfulness are your years of usefulness, so make sense on time. A life without a purpose is a life without meaning.

Chapter 1

Who is a Doctor?

The studies of medicine is very vital in society because of the importance medical doctors possess. World-wide, parents takepride in the fact that their children are either studying or have become qualified Medical Doctors. In each home parents desire that one out of their children should study medicine in higher institution. It is good to continue to encourage young ones to study medicine because they are needed in our society, especial in Africa where thereare brain drains; our finest trained doctors go overseas to look for greener pastures. I pray our leaders will create a conducive environment so that our doctors abroad will come home and contribute to the dying society. Also, Government should provide the needed modern equipment for the doctors to work with or allow private investors to come in, by providing infrastructure for investment.

Medical Doctors are still relevant in our society today world-wide despites the introduction of much technology that could be used to help human health. I believe Doctors are still held in high esteem among the several health practitioners, like the nurses, lab scientist, and pharmacist etc. The current database shows that Nigeria has about 45,000 registered Medical Doctors, and is need of about 155,000 Medical Doctors, so that the ratio between a Doctor and patient will close gap. In Africa as a whole there is need for more qualified Doctors because of the challenges that emerge in the world every day. If the government and the institutions can do the right thing, like giving scholarship and paying the lecturers well, than the country can be exporting our some of our medical doctors to other African countries.

Who is a Doctor? The Picture says it all. A Medical Doctor is a highly responsible individual with high level of professionalism. They are lovely people; with a smile on their faces like the one above, a patient can be assured that he or she will be fine. Medical DoctorsDress code is interesting; they wear an overall, most time white in color. They always appeared sharp as you can see.

Medical doctors are generally physicians who work in clinics, hospitals, medical centers, or private practices. They treat people having injuries or sicknesses. They also prescribe order diagnostic tests, medications, diagnose ailments, and record patients information. Medical Doctors are people orientatedthe love people and care for their patient. They are also full of energy, most time the work round the clock. Always on call

Medical doctors' jobs vary by specialization and work surroundings. Emergency room physicians often will work in fast-pace, highly-stressed environments. However, many family doctors are able to set their own schedules and time in a private medical practice. Helping people in sickness and injury can be very gratifying, but the job requires seriousness and most times carry an emotional toll, as well. A medical Doctor always trusts God for the wisdom and ability to help their patients. Also, the look up to God for the healing and cure of their patients, because they know that God is the number one physician. Doctors must be physically and spiritually balance. A lot of time as a doctors need to pray for their patient while applying medical treatment, to see the total wellbeing of their patient. I believe that not all ailments are normal, some are spiritual, and need the fire power of God to intervene.

Chapter 2

Have a Vision

What is vision: - Vision is a dream, a passion, a picture of a desired future. Any dream or passion that does not have a vision becomes ordinary day dreaming that cannot take you far in life. As young people you need a vision to become **THE DOCTOR**, in life there are medical doctors and there is the medical doctor. The medical doctor is always one of akind, the one that is making a statement in his field, a leader in medical practice, a trail blazer.

Vision is an inspired thought, which takes over you as a person and propels you into an action. Vision comes in the things you like to do, in the things you are doing.

Vision helps you to see far beyond where others cannot see; it makes you work with excellence, above average. Vision = passion = motion = acceleration in life, according to my father in the Lord Dr. Pastor Paul Enenche

Why the vision of medicine: - If you have passion to study medicine, it is a good thing to do. In this time, season, and generation that we are faced with a lot of outbreak of disease, epidemics and all manner of illness and injuries, etc. Then you have work to do, settle down and focus on your studies. You require direction on the subjects to offer in your Ordinary level. Afterprimary school, you have to take your science subject seriously, example like FurtherMathematics, Physic, Chemistry, Biology, Mathematics and English Language. Your Senior Secondary Certificate examination (SSCE) will be a good experience; you will be able to come out with flying colors. Then you are ready for JAMB (that is Joint Admission and Matriculation Board). You have to score high mark to secure admission into the University, your vision to becoming a medical doctor has begun.

Have passion for humanitarian service, help people with their health challenges, body, soul and spirit, then you need God to help in your studies of Medicine. You must realize that human being is made up of spirit, soul and body, as a medical doctor you will not only treat and give prescription to your patient's physical body, but must ensure that you also are able to touch their spirit and their soul.

The stronger your vision the stronger your future, the clearer the vision the clearer the future. If you cannot see where you are going in life, it is an indication that you go nowhere. Life is a product of vision. Vision produces caution, vision produces determination, and vision also produces acceleration in life.

To fulfill your vision you need to be a person of prayer. Because a vision without GOD can lead to frustration, reference God in all you do, He the key to success in life.

To handle vision is to write it down; when you discover your vision, write it down. Things that are written down are not easily forgotten. Vision is to be review from time to time to keep you in remembrance. Finally you need to run with it; it is good to dream but the dream must become a reality for human benefits.

SYLVANUS UDO

Chapter 3

Type Of Medical Doctors And Their Functions

It is important for you to know the different areas of specialization in the studies of medicine. Medicine is very wide but can be major in one aspect. Human body is complex and human life is precious. It entails a lot of details, which is why it is important to major in a particular aspect.

There are lots of the type of medical doctor and their functions. Here we will look at some of them.

1. **Pediatrician**

   Pediatricians are children friendly Doctors. They work with new born baby, children and youth regarding wide range of health matters, infant surfer from common cold to very severe conditions. Children doctors make their work environment highly children friendly.Often featuring colorful painting and interesting arts work, and toys. This is to make the children feel at home and be friendly.

2. **ENT Specialist**

   ENT – E means Ear, N means Nose while T means Throat. This is a specialist area, this area are related or connected to each other. Sometime the earing or smelling condition of the child may be affected and need to be treated, same with the throat, there are related ailment, like pain in the throat, etc.

3. **Epidemiologist**
   Epidemiologists:These are doctors that look out for potential outbreak of disease in the society to prevent it, so that the highest population will not be affected. They look for vaccine to prevent the spread of the disease. Disease such as cancer, HIV/AIDS etc.

4. **Dentist**

   Dentists: A dentists work to ensure dental health. He works with the human mouth, inspecting teeth and gum wellbeing and avoiding and identifyingseveral different problems, such as cavities and bleeding gums. Patients are advised to go to the dentist twice a year in order to sustain tooth health. A lot of people do not know the significance of a Dentist; we should always take advantage of the Dentist, especially for children. Dentist in this part of the world are not taken seriously, people hardly visit the dentist except something serious happen. I never visited the dentist until when I notice that my child's tooth was not forth coming, I had to see the dentist, treatment was conducted and we were advised on what to do. Now my child's complete teeth is out. We now visit the dentist. Tooth disorder in children can be corrected by the dentist.

5. **Neurosurgeon**

Neurosurgeons specialist works on the human brain. He operates on both the brain and body to treat and cure diseases disturbing the nervous system and brain stem. Their operation is torelieve symptoms from serious brain diseases that cause patients a great deal of pains.A woman went through severe pains in the brain;I accompany her to a specialist hospital we were asked to a neurosurgeon thatperforms the necessary surge, now the woman has peace.

6. **Gynecologist**

Gynecologists work with couples, in order to advise them on their reproduction issues either on how or what type of family planning they can adopt etc. Gynecologists work with the female reproductive system to assess and prevent issues that could potentially cause fertility issues. Female patients are typically advised to see a gynecologist once a year. Most couples are ignorance of the fact that Gynecologist can help in better family size. Lack of advice from Gynecologist makes most couples keep taking in, at the end blame themselves or they say it was an accident. No pregnancy is a mistake or an accident, rather two people involve refused to do the right thing at the right time.

7. **Microbiologist**

Microbiologists the are those who study the progress infectious bacteria and viruses and their interactions with the human body to define which could potentially cause damage and break medical conditions. They also seek to find immunizations for diseases caused by these organisms.

8. **Neonatologist**

Neonatologists care for newborn children to safeguard their successful entry into ain good physical shape and fulfilling life. The central point of their examinations is on premature and critically ill babies who needinstant treatment at the threat of mortal consequences.

9. **Physiologist**

Physiologists study the states of the human body, including emotions and needs. They particularly focus on the functions of the human body to assess if they are working correctly and attempt to determine potential problems before they become an issue.

10. Podiatrist

Those who study and work on ailments which afflict feet and patients' ankles are called Podiatrists. Most times, they are referred to as "foot doctors" who treat afflictions like athlete's foot, nail disorders, calluses, and commonly known foot infections and injuries.

11. Obstetrician

Obstetricians work with child birth. They are trained to handle child birth and pregnancy, especially when a woman is in labour. They ensure general wellbeing of the child and mother. Operations related to female reproductive system are also performed by them.

12. Oncologist

Some experts focus on the prevention and treatment of cancer regarding terminal and risk prone patients, these set of people are called Oncologists. They provide medical care for a person who as been diagnose with cancer, chemotherapy and radiotherapy capable of destroying cancer cells found in the body, including follow-up with survivors after treatment successes.

13. Psychiatrist

Psychiatrists occupy a more prevailing place in field of research than medical field. They study mental and behaviors processes and often work on patients by one-on-one sessions alleviating mental illnesses and behavioral disorders, with lot of mental problem in Nigeria and Africa as a whole. Young people engage in drugs abuse which leads to mental problem. The use of drugs must be checked by relevant authority, to reduce this menace.

14. Radiologist

Radiologists use x-rays and other facilities such as imaging technologies to diagnose and detect physiological ailments. They carry this out by scanning victim's body for all hazardous cells, including cancer cells, and also look for breaks or fractures in accident victims.

15. Urologist

Urologists are experts in matters related to urinary system, including urinary tract infections. Also, they study and treat afflictions of kidneys, bladder, adrenal glands and the male reproductive organs.

16. Gastroenterologists

Gastroenterologists deal with stomach and intestinal issues. They are doctor who studies diseases related to the digestive system and also gives treatment connected to the gastroenterology.

17. Dermatologist

Dermatologists examine patients to test for such

risk factors like basal cell carcinoma (that signals skin cancer) also moles that may ultimately cause skin disease if not treated quickly. Essentially, Dermatologists study skin and the associated structures, functions and diseases associated with it.

Cardiologists

Cardiologists are doctors that specialize in heart, so diagnose and treat heart diseases. Cardiologists study the human heart and many diseases and issues related to it and offer appropriate treatment. They look through the medical and family history of the patients to determine likely potential risk of certain cardiovascular diseases and take special action to check them.

18. Orthopedic Surgeon

Orthopedic Surgeons treat bones disorder; also specialize in hip, knee, and ankle. These doctors are frequently found in emergency rooms as accidents resulting in broken bones are habitually unintentional placed there and demand immediate treatment. Orthopedic surgeon may be the highest paid doctor.

SYLVANUS UDO

How Much Doctors Actually Make

Doctors are compensated according to the peculiar nature of their specialty.

In our recent outcome from medical resource Medscape, just came out with its 2016 Doctors Compensation Report, which features data from more than 19,200 doctors in 26 specialties. All the data is self-reported and based on information collected for Medscape's yearly survey.

There are some Doctors that are highly paid and those that are lowest paid in the profession as shown below in the Medscape.

Take a look at the graphic below to see the average earnings for doctors from each specialty:

HOW MUCH MONEY PHYSICIANS MAKE

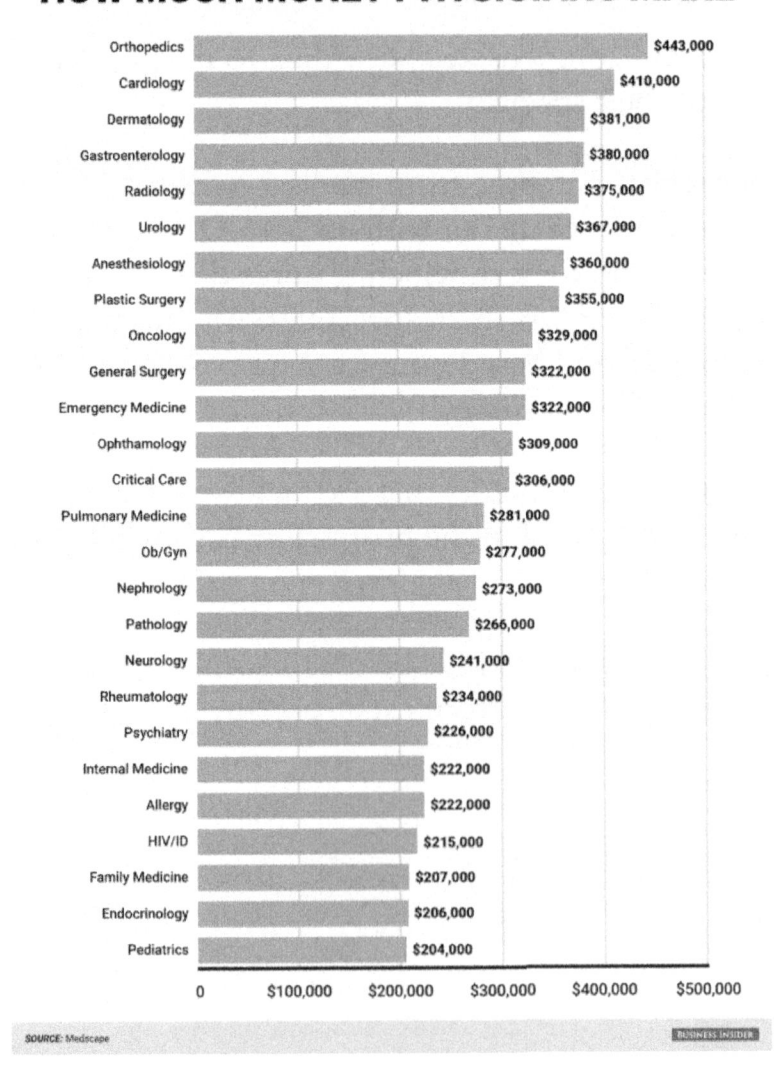

Orthopedics	$443,000
Cardiology	$410,000
Dermatology	$381,000
Gastroenterology	$380,000
Radiology	$375,000
Urology	$367,000
Anesthesiology	$360,000
Plastic Surgery	$355,000
Oncology	$329,000
General Surgery	$322,000
Emergency Medicine	$322,000
Ophthamology	$309,000
Critical Care	$306,000
Pulmonary Medicine	$281,000
Ob/Gyn	$277,000
Nephrology	$273,000
Pathology	$266,000
Neurology	$241,000
Rheumatology	$234,000
Psychiatry	$226,000
Internal Medicine	$222,000
Allergy	$222,000
HIV/ID	$215,000
Family Medicine	$207,000
Endocrinology	$206,000
Pediatrics	$204,000

SOURCE: Medscape / BUSINESS INSIDER

Chapter 4

Medical Instrument And Their Uses

STETHOSCOPES

The are used to hear sounds from movements within the body like heart beats, intestinal movement, breath sounds, etc. It is part of the Medical Doctor's dress coat.

SYRINGE AND NEEDLES

It is used for injections and aspiration of blood or fluid from the body

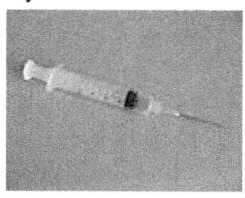

BANDAGE

Used to cover and protect area of the body that may have recent injures

First Aid box

First Aid box is very important, is used to administer to injured person first before the Doctor's examination.

SPHYGMOMANOMETER

This is used for measuring the level of blood pressure. A doctor measures blood pressure by observing the meter on the sphygmomanometer, while simultaneously listening with a stethoscope to the changing sounds produced by the blood flow in the compressed artery in the arm.

OTOSCOPE

Good lighting is a basic requirement when examining any region of the human body. An examination room requires good general lighting. In addition to this, an examination light increases the amount of light in the area being inspected.

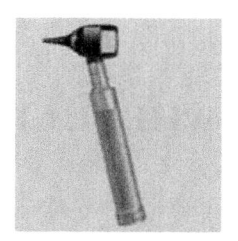

THEMOMETER

It is used in measuring the temperature of the body.

This type is a digital thermometer

HAND GLOVE

Examination gloves serve as a two-way barrier to reduce the risk of transferring potentially harmful microorganisms
Between patient and doctor or other healthcare workers. A thorough washing and drying of the hands using soap and water is essential before putting on examination gloves. Different sized hands require specific sized gloves. Disposable.

WHEEL CHAIR

Wheel chair is used to wheel a patient who cannot walk on his own, to see the doctor or where he can receive treatment.

PAN OF BLOOD

Blood is very important for life. We are encouraged by the Health Centre to always donate blood, to be stored in blood bank. Especially when it is emergency situation patient are in need of blood to save their life.

Chapter 5

Why Do People Consult Medical Doctors

Nobody likes going to the doctor, but every year thousands of people go through the effort of setting up an appointment just to get checked up. Why? Some people just want to make sure they're generally in good health, so they take a little preventative action with a doctor visit. In this part of my world, I have noticed that people don't have the culture of visiting or consulting a doctor when their condition is still manageable, they wait until the situation becomes worst untilthey are rushed to health Centre to see doctor.

Others though, visit for their body maintenance, to make sure there is nothing hiding in their body system. I believe consulting a doctor should be a life style, say once or twice every a year, you should go for checkup, we shouldn't wait until the situation become critical before we consult the doctor. It is cheaper to always consult the doctor or make it a life style to visit doctor when you still feel strong and healthy. Some have a specific reason for visiting the doctor, and it's because they're sick. Sick with one ailment or the other.

Sometimes, it is in emergency situation that people visit doctor. When you think about it, there could be lots, hundreds, or even thousands of diseases/illnesses that'd cause somebody to go to the doctor.

In fact, you can probably guess the most common illnesses right off the bat; just ask yourself "what illnesses do I see regularly among friends and family?" What do they complain about all the time? Colds? Headaches? What?

As a matter of fact, it's quite likely that you yourself have experienced at least a few of these symptoms. That's how common these diseases/illnesses are, so don't be surprised if you find yourself saying "I have had that problem!"

6

Importance And Duties Of Medical Doctors

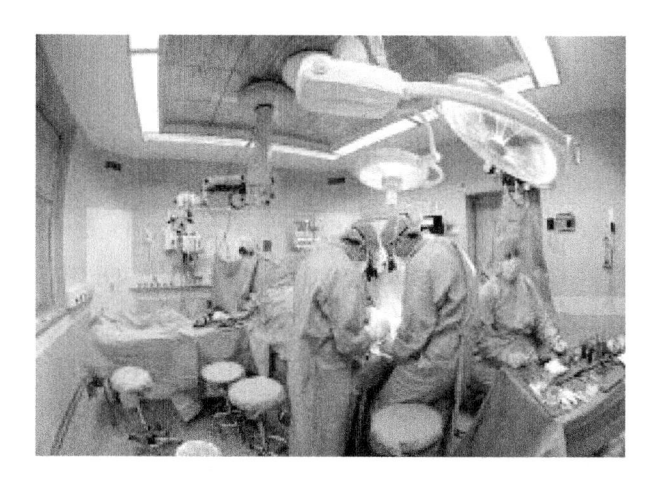

A doctor has responsibility for providing professional health care services to patients. Before the discovery of modern medicine, life was fleeting for humans. The environment was replete with unseen dangers in the form of disease and medical conditions. Then medical practice changed into an organized profession, and humans experienced a significant improvement in the quality of life. Aided by modern scientific innovation, the boundaries of medical technology extended to unimaginable limits. Nevertheless, even with all these technological innovations, the position of doctors in society hasn't reduced; doctors remain necessary.

These are the few point that shows the importance and duties of medical doctors in the society. These include the following:-

1. **Saving Lives**

The main purpose of doctors is to save life. I feel disappointed when hospital refused to treat a patient because of issue of money. In certain conditions, a doctor can mean the difference between life and death. Accident and violent crime victims and soldiers wounded on the battlefield know this because their lives rest on the skills of surgeons. People who suffer critical injuries need a doctor to attend to them quickly because delaying treatment might simply mean death. A pregnant woman who is in labour and it has become critical and complicated need a quick intervention of doctor to bring fort, for both lives to be preserved.

2. **Extending Life**

Doctors are responsible for better life expectancy and improved well-being in society. People who survive diseases such as cancer usually owe their survival to God and doctors, whose skills and dedication are vital for their cure. Modern medical technology coupled with doctors' care can give a persons diagnosed with terminal illnesses hope of living longer. There are many people who have this testimony about a terminal illness that look like their life was finished but through the help of God and our tireless Doctors that illness was terminated from their system.

3. Humanitarian Work

Doctors perform humanitarian work in society. Some advocacy groups on health issues, such as hypertension and cancer, draw membership from the medical profession and help spread information about how to avoid so-called lifestyle diseases. Doctors may work as volunteers on missions ranging from providing care to disaster victims to training medical personnel in the developing world. Most times, these doctors go to the urban area, the interior village where there are no doctors, especially in Africa to provide free medical service.

4. Monitoring Epidemics and Conducting Research.

When disease outbreaks occur, information provided by doctors can help hold the epidemic. They also check the spread of disease by alerting the public to factors, such as poor hygiene and risky behaviors, which spread disease. Doctors also work alongside researchers to find new cures for diseases, running drug tests on consenting patients.

The Duties Of Doctors In The Society

Doctors have many duties toward their patients. Their responsibilities cover their own actions, as well as orders they give to their assistants, such as nurses, medical students and residents.

These are a doctor's main duties:

1. Treat the admitted Patients

When a patient is admitted in the hospital, the doctor has the obligation to conduct treatment. The treatment must be at the right time. The patient need to be relieve of pains.
They must treat their patients attentively and conscientiously.

Doctors must recognize their own limits: in case of doubt, they must get information from other people or refer patients to specialists.

The duty to treat patients includes the duty to

- prescribe the right medication,
- tell patients about the proposed treatment or operation, and
- Provide adequate follow-up to the patient within a reasonable amount of time.

For example, after a treatment, a doctor must provide the medical follow-up required by the patient's state of health, or at least make sure that a colleague or other professional follows up.

2. Provision of right Information

Doctors must give their patients all the information they need to make free and informed decisions. For example, doctors must tell their patients about the following:

- diagnosis
- nature, goal and seriousness of the treatment
- risks of the treatment

The doctor's duty to provide information also includes answering patients' questions.

The doctor's duty is toward the patients themselves, the people who make decisions on behalf of patients, or the parents of children under the age of 14. Doctors must explain the chances of success and the risk of failure of the suggested treatment, keeping in mind the patient's specific condition.

Doctors must also inform their patients about the possible negative effect of a treatment. However, it is impossible for a doctor to talk about all of the possible risks; doctors must tell their patients about the foreseeable risks, in other words the risks that are most likely to occur. Doctors must also tell patients about any rare risk that could have serious consequences. The extent of the duty to provide information depends on the circumstances and the patient in question.

For some types of treatments, doctors are required to give more complete and specific information about the risks. This is the case, for example, with purely experimental treatments as well as treatments that are not aimed at curing an illness or injury, like some types of plastic surgery. In these cases, doctors must tell patients about all possible and rare risks.

3. Ensure Patient is Willing To Gives Free and Informed Consent

The purpose behind the duty of doctors to provide information to patients is to give patients all the information they need to make free and informed decisions with full knowledge of the facts about the treatment and care offered. When a patient agrees to treatment or care, this is called consent.
The duty to get the consent of patients is a continuous process. This is why patients must be kept informed about any new information about their states of health and the treatments they are receiving.

4. Respect Of Privacy

Doctors have a responsibility to respect their patients' privacy. This is sometimes called the duty of professional secrecy.
This responsibility covers both the information patients tell their doctors and any truths doctors discover about

their patients as part of the doctor-patient relationship.

Professional secrecy belongs to the patient, not the doctor. Doctors cannot disclose what their patients tell them, unless their patients surrender the confidentiality of the information or if the law allows it. For example, the *Public Health Act* says that certain diseases must be reported to public health agencies.

Chapter 7

Common Illnessess, Deases And Infections/Symptoms

Headache:-Headache is the symptom of pain anywhere in the region of the head . There is also an increased risk of depression in those with severe headaches.Primary headaches are stand-alone illnesses which are caused directly by the over activity of, or problems with, structures in the head that are**pain**-sensitive.

Body pains: -General body pains are a sign that the body is dealing with a condition that is affecting the body as a whole. Body pains are typically an immune response to an infection or condition that needs to be addressed in order for the pain to stop. General body aches are typically a sign that your body is feeling down. In many cases this pain is dull and will resolve itself on its own. In other cases this is a response from the immune system that is letting the body know that something is causing a disturbance. This can be an infection or an injury. Noting the other symptoms that accompany the aches and pains will help you determine the underlying cause so it can be properly treated.

Symptoms of General Body Aches

Body aches are rarely severe. They will manifest themselves as a general aching sensation or stiffness throughout the body. In some cases this can be described as a burning or searing pain. This may also be accompanied by weakness, low endurance, sleep disturbances and fatigue. Conditions such as travelling long distances, muscular extension, and humidity, alteration in barometric pressure or emotional stress can have an impact on the presence of these symptoms.

Cold and cough: -It usually begins with a sore throat, and before you know it, you've also got these symptoms:

- Runny nose (clear and watery)
- Sneezing
- Fatigue
- Cough

You usually don't get a fever with a cold. If you do, it may be a sign you've got the malaria or an infection with a bacteria.

For the first few days that you're sick, your runny nose will be watery, but it turns thicker and darker after that. You may also get a mild cough that can last into the second week of your cold.

Since a cold can make your asthma worse, check with your doctor to see if you need to change your regular treatment plan.

If you cough up thick or dark mucus or you get a fever, you may have an infection with bacteria. See your doctor to find out how to treat it. Also see him if your cough doesn't get better after a few weeks.

Your symptoms usually start between 1 and 3 days after you get infected with a cold virus. They typically last for about 3 to 7 days. By then the worst is over, but you may feel stuffed up for a week or more.

You're most contagious during the first 3 days that you're sick, but it's still possible to spread it during the first week.

Fever/Malaria: -As the malaria parasites enter the blood stream they infect and destroy red blood cells. Destruction of these essential cells leads to fever and malaria-like symptoms, such as chills, headache, muscle aches, tiredness, nausea, vomiting and diarrhea. These initial symptoms are non-specific: in other words, they are self-reported symptoms that do not indicate a specific disease process.

Allergies: - Common symptoms of an allergic reaction include:

- sneezing and an itchy, runny or blocked nose (allergic rhinitis)
- itchy, red, watering eyes (conjunctivitis)
- Wheezing, chest tightness, shortness of breath and a cough.
- a raised, itchy, red rash (hives)
- Swollen lips, tongue, eyes or face.
-

Asthma: -

A respiratory condition characterized by attacks of spasm in the bronchi part of the lungs, leading to difficulty in breathing. It is usually connected to allergic reaction or other forms of hypersensitivity.

The most frequent symptoms of asthma are:

- Coughing, especially in the night, during an exercise or when laughing.
- Difficulty breathing.
- Chest tightness.
- Shortness of breath

Diarrhea:-

Diarrhea may be followed by cramping, abdominal pain, nausea, a pressing need to use the bathroom, or loss of bowel control. Some infections that cause diarrhea can also cause a fever and chills or bloody stools.

Dehydration

Diarrhea can cause dehydration. Loss of electrolytes through dehydration affects the amount of water in the body, muscle exercise, and other vital functions.

Dehydration is particularly dangerous among older adults, children, and people known with weakened immune systems. Dehydration need to be treated quickly to avoid serious health problems, such as organ damage, shock, or coma—a sleeplike state in which a person is not conscious.

Signs of dehydration in adults include

- thirst
- less frequent urination than usual
- dry skin
- fatigue
- dizziness
- light-headedness

Signs of dehydration in infants and young children include

- dry mouth and tongue
- no tears when crying
- no wet diapers in 3 hours or more
- high fever

Chapter 8

Keys To Achieving What You Want In Life

1. **Desire:** it is what you desire as a person that can become your own, how badly do you want it. Students who just gain admission into the University and desire to graduate with first class, it is possible for him or her to achieve it. There is difference between **desire** and **want,** desire is stronger than want, it does not matter how much you want a thing if the desire is not there, the will power become very weak.
2. **Decision:** Your decision in life is important to what you want to be in life. A person of decision is a person of destination. Your decision can either make you or break you. Making the right decision in life is not a luxury but a necessity. When you discover your passion in life make up your mind to pursue it. Procrastinationset in because of indecision and to will power to do what you need to

achieve. There can be no delivery without a quality decision.

3. **Direction:** To know direction is to know progress in life and divine direction also bring speed, delay is arrested through direction. When you know where to go, your journey is not prolong in life. Direction is inside into the way of achieving purpose in life and destiny.

4. **Diligence:** The combination of intellectual and physical activities, the willingness to work until it is work out. The care and perseverance required in a work to bringing out the desire result. A person who is diligent in his or her work definitely will be shifted higher in life. Putting in extra time and effort in what you do,that can distinguish you. Diligent is a cure for hard life.

5. **Determination**: how far are you willing to go.Be determine to get there, the journey is normally not smooth, so you need determination to reach your destination. What is your mind set towards what you want to achieve in life. It is staying power, strong mindedness, positive doggedness, courageousness and bravery, steadfastness in pursue of what you want to achieve in life.

6. **Discipline**: The willingness to pay the price for what you want. Discipline is a raw material for successful destiny, the higher you want to fly the higher the price you have to pay. To be discipline is to be molded to behave in certain way. Discipline preserves character and character is the way to the top. Discipline will take you far in life. Your discipline is your determination to do what is right. The ability to say no to unprofitable life.

7. **Dedication: B**e dedicated to God, your work. Dedication determines commitment to duties, and focus to work. Some time we abandon what we started halt way. Procrastination also denies us of dogged dedication and commitment to our God given vision. If you want to be successful in life be dedicated to your calling.

Chapter 9

Exercise on Human body

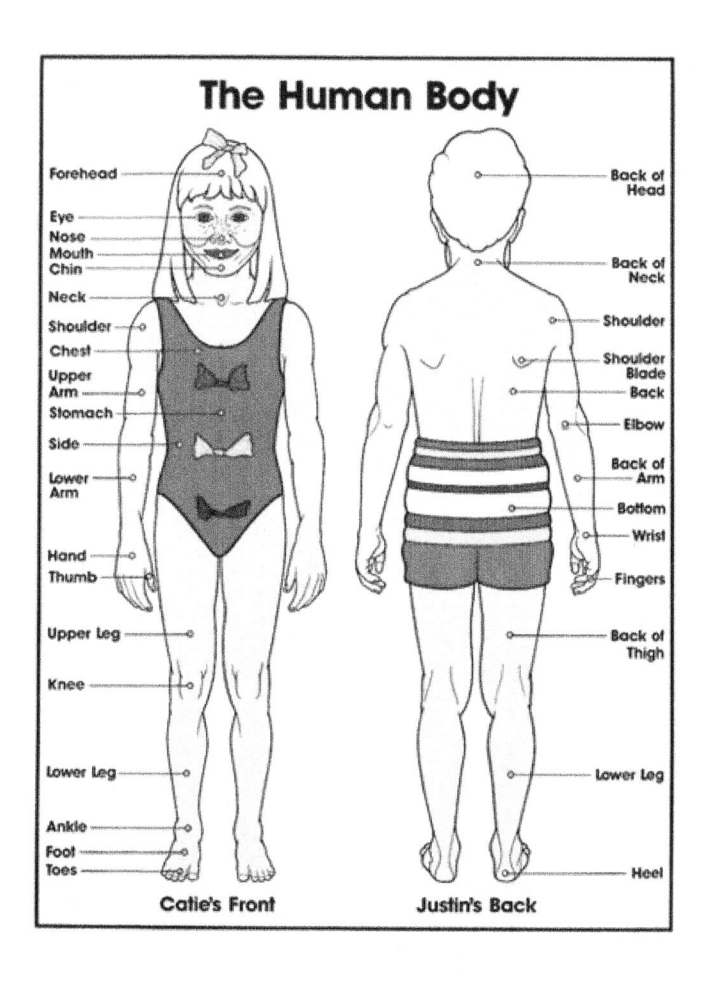

The Human Body

Forehead
Eye
Nose
Mouth
Chin
Neck
Shoulder
Chest
Upper Arm
Stomach
Side
Lower Arm
Hand
Thumb
Upper Leg
Knee
Lower Leg
Ankle
Foot
Toes

Back of Head
Back of Neck
Shoulder
Shoulder Blade
Back
Elbow
Back of Arm
Bottom
Wrist
Fingers
Back of Thigh
Lower Leg
Heel

Catie's Front   **Justin's Back**

Some body parts name have got jumbled up, rewrite them correctly

yees　　　　　_____

raes　　　　　_____

plis　　　　　_____

achtoms　　　_____

anhd　　　　 _____

earht　　　　_____

ootf　　　　　_____

gutnoe　　　 _____

osen　　　　 _____

ungls　　　　_____

I WANT TO BE A DOCTOR

Name _____

My Body Worksheet

Look at the picture of the boy below and use the word bank at the bottom of the page to help you label the different parts of the body.

Word bank: Hair Eye Leg Hand Arm Nose Mouth Shoulder Ear Knee Elbow Foot

About The Book

I want to be a Doctor is packaged specifically for children and youth and our distinguished parents who are in love with the profession. This book is to continue to encourage young people to take up the medical profession as career. Most of the children I have encounter, when asked what they want to become in future 85% of them would respond they want to be a Doctor. Obviously, a Medical Doctor not a native doctor.

Printed in Great Britain
by Amazon